HOW TO DRAW
WILD ANIMALS
OF THE COUNTRYSIDE

HOW TO DRAW

other titles in this series

HOW TO DRAW
WILD ANIMALS
OF THE COUNTRYSIDE

by W. S. HUNTER

THE STUDIO PUBLICATIONS

London & New York

First published 1954

MY THANKS ARE DUE TO
Clifford Musgrave, Director of Brighton Museum
and Ronald Sansom, Curator of Peterborough Private Museum
for allowing me to make use of their galleries and exhibits
for study :
to D. A. Wimble, Principal of Horsham School of Art for
facilities for drawing and modelling animals :
to W. R. Harris, who allowed me to wander at will over his land
and study the native fauna, for his help on the badger and the
fox and the many items of knowledge and interest exchanged in
conversation : and last but decidedly not least,
to my father who inculcated and encouraged a love of
natural history and drawing

Published in London by The Studio Limited, 66 Chandos Place, WC2
and in New York by Studio Publications Inc, 432 Fourth Avenue ;
printed in England by Bradford and Dickens, Drayton House, London, WC1

CONTENTS

INTRODUCTION

WHEN the idea of this book first occurred to me I determined that I would include only those animals which I had seen and had been able to study at first hand. Therefore, neither the pine-martin nor the pole-cat will appear within its pages. Both of these may still exist but are so rare as to be virtually extinct in Britain. For the same reason I have excluded the harvest mouse. I have not seen one myself for over twenty years and I can find no one who has seen one for a very long time.

The only partial exception I have made is in the matter of the wild cat. I have never seen this splendid animal free and in its native haunts. A friend, curator of a private museum in Peterborough, had two very fine specimens sent him and it is from these that the sketches in this book are derived.

Regarding the word 'animal'. Many people confuse this with 'mammal'. A mammal is distinct from other animals in that it has hair on its body, external ears and mammaries for suckling its young (which are born alive and not from eggs).

Animals include all those living, breathing organisms which are not plants : this includes even the amoeba and the microbe.

It is not out of place, therefore to include in this book a few of the more commonly known insects, the amphibians and that interesting and beautifully patterned ophidian, the British viper.

APPROACH TO DRAWING

IN DRAWING the native animals of Britain, there are two problems that immediately confront us. First, *where to find them:* Secondly, *when found they do not keep still.* No other subject presents two such formidable obstacles. When drawing animals in captivity, the first does not exist at all and the second only partially, for the area of their movement is limited and quite often they will rest and sleep in full view.

With domesticated animals too, the problem is not nearly so acute. Their range is larger than that of a caged animal, but their movements are, generally speaking, lethargic and they are accustomed to Man.

Problems, however, were made to be solved and this book is *my* solution. You will be able to develop it or perhaps find a better.

Some small knowledge of natural history is desirable. You will then, knowing the habits of a creature, be able to deduce its habitat. And as your knowledge increases you will not only know what to look for, but what you are looking *at*.

It is astonishing what a large number of tell-tale signs one can find with just a little background knowledge. What were thought to be rabbit runs will, to the more experienced eye prove to be badger-runs. Large holes in banks may be foxes' earths, or even badgers' sets. The latter are distinguishable by the really enormous amount of soil disturbed and—irrefutable evidence—the rolls of bracken and grass, which is their bedding, out to dry.

Regarding problem number two, it is safe to say that no wild animal will stay long enough for you to make a complete drawing of it.

The wild animals of Britain are a shy, retiring lot. The needs of an intensive agricultural system combined with the increasing urbanisation have meant their persecution to such an extent that their lives depend upon their ability to avoid man.

We must come upon them already armed with some knowledge of their form and the ability to express it. Thus we shall be able to devote our time to observing the *significant* lines, curves and shapes of their movements.

This foreknowledge may be obtained in more than one way and the greater number of sources we explore the wider our vocabulary and the more varied our selection.

The first source has already been mentioned. In solving our first problem by acquiring a knowledge of natural history we have started to solve problem number two. Some knowledge of anatomy and physiology will have been gained and this will prove a great asset when we start to draw from life.

The second and which I feel to be the most valuable source, is the museum. Here are the actual animals 'in the round', immobilized for us and we may study them at our leisure and from every angle.

Do not, however, just enter a museum and start to sketch ! It is only courteous to ask permission. I have never had a request refused.

It is important to make some study of the bony structure and perhaps individual drawings of the main limb-bones and joints. By so doing you will rapidly gain a knowledge of the limb's movements and limits and the reason for the animal's habitual stance.

A comprehensive knowledge of anatomy or osteology is not required. It does not matter if you do not know the name of a single bone, though some nomenclature will inevitably be acquired in the process. As long as you know the functions of the main bones, the shapes of the main musculature, that is all that is required.

Remember, the bones are the armature upon which the muscles depend and together they are responsible for the external planes, the folds and the undulations of the skin.

The third source is photographs. Working from these presents its own problems and it is, perhaps, a somewhat unsatisfactory method but one that cannot be overlooked. Photographs are honest, not 'true' representations of an animal for an instant of time. But their shadows are usually vague and their lightest portions without the subtle nuances that will give life to even a poorly representational drawing. However, they can prove of value and should not be omitted.

Another source is the work of other artists. Much has been written about the dangers of studying another person's methods : the words 'copying' and 'self-expression' have been used copiously and largely erroneously.

Self-expression is a very good thing, a most desirable ultimate goal. But it is an *ultimate* goal : not an immediate one. Most of the really great artists did quite a deal of ' copying ', that is studying the work of previous painters and seeking to discover how they obtained their effects.

As for copying from nature, one cannot ! It is impossible to copy the colour of the sky, to show each twig on a tree, each leaf, But by paying close attention to such things, by *trying to copy them as exactly as possible* one can learn the essentials of their form, what is important in their shapes, the *significance* of their form.

A composer does not write music until he has learnt to read a score : a bricklayer does not build a house until he has learnt how to place bricks so that they cohere and are plumb. And they both need to study other people's work and learn something of their methods before they can start to work on their own. And with drawing it is no different.

I am well aware that drawing is an individual thing. No two people will see the same object in exactly the same way, but it should be obvious that the wider one's knowledge of methods and techniques the greater one's ability to express one's *own* interpretation of a subject.

But all these sources from which to obtain an initial knowledge are useless—I repeat, useless—unless one also draws from the living model. The work of other artists, museums, photographs, these will give you a base from which to start, an idea of what to look for, but that is all.

It is this question of what to look for that is so important in drawing. It is quite a time before one can really 'see' one's subject, the constructional lines beneath the outer form, the rhythmic patterns and important planes.

Strangely enough it is not these vital things that one sees when starting to draw from nature, but all the little unimportant details. The eye is led astray by all sorts of trivial shapes and lines.

Drawing wild animals from life can be done in two ways. On sighting one's subject one can whip out a sketch-book and try to get somthing down before the quarry vanishes. Or one can observe and try to memorise. If one follows the former method it is fairly certain the subject will vanish even more precipitately. All one will get in most cases will be a blurred impression on the retina and nothing on the paper. Of course this does not apply to such creatures as frogs and toads, snails etc. Though the best way of drawing even these is to imprison them for a time in a glass jar.

Very occasionally an animal will, though frequently changing its position, keep within sight so that you can get down several quick impressions. I have been able to draw snakes when the first warmth has drawn them from winter hibernation and they are still partly comatose Among mammals, I have drawn stoats direct from life. A stoat is intensely curious and determined. I have had one watch me from a distance and then make a detour to get a closer view.

I have little doubt, however, that the second method is the better. To use every available second for observing, noting and memorising the vital shapes and forms the animal makes in its movements. Keep still, do not move, especially the hands or arms and you will be surprised how close to you the wary creatures of wood and field will come. Then, when they have gone, you can immediately set down your impressions. Your basic training of drawing the skeletal forms and fixed poses in the museums will now stand you in good stead. Not only in developing those swift impressions, but by enabling you to *see* the fundamental structure in the living animal.

Drawing from 'memory' is, on analysis, no different from any other way of drawing. In fact one *always* draws from memory, even when the model is still in front of one. Each time you look at the model and then at your paper to draw what you have seen you are carrying a visual image of the subject *in your memory*.

True, when the model is stationary one can refresh the memory at extremely short intervals, but with practice it will be found that the period of 'remembrance' can be lengthened to an astonishing degree.

MATERIALS

I AM not going to discuss these at any length. There are many excellent papers etc on the market and by experience you will find those best suited to your individual taste. This may take a little while but it will not be in any way a waste of time. You will gain valuable experience and knowledge that is beyond the power of any book to give.

The majority of the drawings in this book were made with a 2B pencil on ordinary cartridge paper. Now and then I have used a softer pencil. When a drawing under discussion was made with anything other than these materials I have noted it in the relevant text.

CONSTRUCTION · THE BADGER AS AN EXAMPLE

No DRAWING will be worth while unless the basic construction is vigorous and well founded. Unless the major planes and significant lines are in proper relationship, all fitting into a harmonious whole, the result will be disappointing.

It is necessary that separate parts of the anatomy should be studied and detailed drawings made, but unless the previous statement is fully realised and carried out, the finished work will be weak and unsatisfactory. An animal is a cohesion of those parts and no one part may be developed at the expense of the whole drawing.

Therefore, start with the major planes. The basic structure of all mammals is the same, only the proportions differ according to the specific use of the limb or organ.

This foreshortened drawing of the badger's head shows its resemblance to the pig and the bear.
The eyes too are pig-like and small but low down towards the snout.
We can see then that more than one mammal may be indicated in a single species

13

The badger is a member of the weasel family, but the family characteristics, the sinuous lines and undulating movement are not easily discernible. Rather does it show those traits that have earned it the pseudonym of 'the English bear'. It has a rolling shambling gait, a propensity to turn in its toes, and a shaggy lumpy-looking bulk.

In addition to these features, it also possesses some which, with its habits, have earned it another name, 'earth-pig'. In fact the male is known as a boar and the female a sow.

Let me repeat that the underlying structure of all mammals is the same. The figure below shows in diagrammatic form the main bony structure of any mammal. I have purposely left out the ribs. These main bones are : skull ; backbone ; shoulder blade or scapula ; upper arm or humerus ; forearm consisting of two bones, the ulna and the radius ; wrist bones or carpus ; hand bones or metacarpus ; fingers or phalanges ; hip bones or sacrum ; thigh bone or femur ; the leg bones,

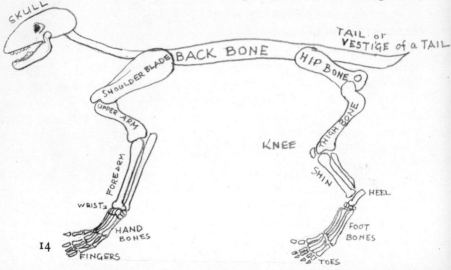

A badger has five claws on each foot, those on the fore-feet being the larger for digging. The claws are arranged in an almost straight line, not in a curve round the foot as in the dog or the fox. When walking it places one foot in front of the other so that its track is in an almost straight line too.

footprint of a badger

footprint of a fox

the tibia and the fibula ; the small bones at the end of the leg and heel (or tarsus) ; foot bones or metatarsus ; toes or phalanges.

In the skeleton of the badger on this page you will notice how flat the metacarpals lie. This is the reason for the badger's flat-footed shuffle and differentiates him from those animals which walk on their toes (digitigrades) such as the fox, cat, dog, or the tip-toe walkers (ungulates) such as the horse and the ass.

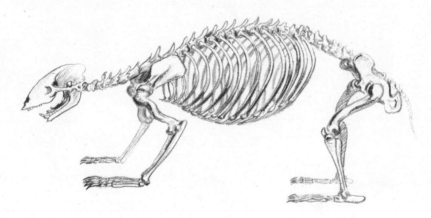

The skeleton of a badger and, *opposite*, the main bony structure without the ribs

An obstacle to delineating form is a rough shaggy coat. Any animal that shows a definite line of body and limb is always easier to draw. If you doubt this try drawing a greyhound and then have a shot at one of those squat, shapeless little dogs that do not get enough exercise !

It is for this very reason, the difficulty of seeing the structural shape beneath the long coarse hair, that I have chosen the badger for our first example. His loose coat hides the modelling beneath, but once you know the main planes of the body-mass then you can discern them beneath the shapeless exterior.

The varying planes of the body-mass beneath the loose hair. These major planes should never be lost sight of or the modelling will suffer.

Right : a more subtle form with the exaggerated cubist form of the planes softened, but with the definite shapes still over-emphasised for your guidance.

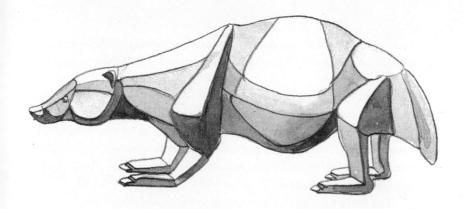

Always keep these basic forms in mind. The fall of the hair will largely follow the bumps and hollows which lie along the planes beneath, just as grass must follow the undulations of the ground below and, according to the angle of light, reflect it in greater or lesser degree.

Let your pencil strokes follow as nearly as possible the contours that you know lie beneath. Make your lines follow the line of growth, curl over the bulges and into the depressions, with lessening pressure for the former and a harder one for the latter.

Of course, one may hatch, or cross-hatch when and where necessary.

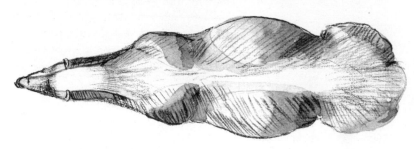

As a general rule it is wiser to let your pencil strokes follow the natural form : experience will show when it is necessary to depart from general rules.

Try to find these features in whatever animal you are drawing. Look for them and draw them in, boldly and exaggeratedly. As your drawing proceeds they will lose their sharp definition. So if you have not put them in boldly and firmly at first, by the time you have finished your work they will have disappeared entirely. Do not be afraid of over-emphasis in this respect.

The badger is one of those animals that you will *not* be able to draw from life on the spot. The slightest movement or scent will put him down. He is the shyest and most retiring of all our fauna. Most museums have a stuffed specimen of Brock, or you may be lucky enough to know someone who has a tame one as a pet. But if you cannot draw him from life in his natural surroundings you can, with a little discomfort to yourself perhaps, observe him. He is quite common, though not often seen because of his excessively wary nature.

Almost any large wood, preferably on sandy soil and not too far from water will shelter one and perhaps two colonies.

The best time for seeing him is undoubtedly the spring. He usually comes out about dusk and being a creature of habit, tends to emerge at approxi-

A badger emerging from his hole.
The uneven ground
accentuates the rolling gait.

mately the same time as the previous evening. So that in June, when the light remains appreciably longer on successive evenings, he can often be seen just before it is really dusk.

Badger's head,
showing the long
tapering snout

Back three-quarter view, showing the
very bear-like attitude.
From this angle even the head has an ursine look

Badger at a pool.
This shows the awkward stance often adopted
by the animal—the turned-in toes
and the heavy lumpishness of the body

Studies in charcoal and Conté pencil. Above is a tone drawing, that is line is not used to denote shape, but a picture is built up by tones, dark against light mass. The antithesis of this style of drawing can be seen on pages 26, 27, 40 and 41. I shall have more to say about that later.

As the badger is usually seen at night, the landscape appears darker than the animal. Generally speaking, Brock first appears as a grey blur at the black mouth of his tunnel. It is only when he comes out into the open, and by staring fixedly at him, that one can discover the form. In actual observation of him in the wild, the legs are not conspicuous.

When the badger sharpens his claws, much as a cat does, on a tree trunk, his resemblance to cousin otter is clear.

This is a sketch-book impression.

The two further badgers show the unmistakeable lines of the weasel, whose close relative they are. There is, at all times, a particularly boneless look about all members of the weasel family. The near one exemplifies that squat shapeless, almost legless look a badger has when viewed in the precincts of its home.

THE WEASEL

I CHOSE the badger to commence because in his form can be seen not only the characteristics of the family (Mustelidae) but superficial and easily recognizable resemblances to other mammals It may help us to appreciate that the underlying pattern of all mammals is the same.

Having therefore dealt with that member which shows least the family traits we will now examine one that shows them most clearly.

The weasel is a long lithe undulating cylinder on four short legs. If you you remember this and keep it as the dominant form, you will realise its true character.

Although it has only the normal number of cervical vertebrae (seven) it is difficult to tell externally where the body ends and the neck begins. The whole body has a rippling snake-like motion.

The charcoal drawings opposite show the underlying principles of its construction and that whatever position it is in this pattern remains true.

Often when one has just glimpsed one's subject a few lines drawn immediately in the sketch-book will convey a sense of vitality and movement that the more ' finished ' drawing lacks. On pages 24 and 25 are some of these jottings taken from a small sketch-book that I am never without.

The most that one can hope for from these scribbles is to get down some of the significant lines and, in fact, that is all that is necessary.

It is the ability to recognize the significant lines and planes that we must constantly cultivate.

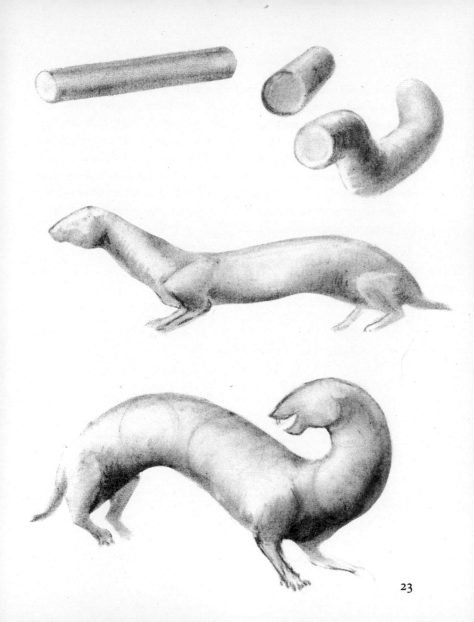

There is nothing lumpy or bulging about a weasel, therefore let your line be a smooth one, fluid and largely unbroken. Breaks at tail and joints are not unpleasing. In fact they will give vitality to your line. But generally speaking, the one word that (to my mind) expresses that smooth ripple of ferocity known as the weasel, is 'continuity'. There are no ponderous muscles on haunches or shoulders, nothing to break the continuous line from tip of the nose to end of the short tail. Even a snake is not such an example of homogenity, for often its patterning will break its visual lines.

25

Here are two drawings of weasels. On the left the animal is bunched, a posture it assumes when attacked or startled. Below, a more familiar stance : notice how the lines follow the form and not only give the solidity but suggest the underlying structure

26

THE STOAT

This is another member of the family and very much akin to the weasel. It has been said that as the stoat is totally different, you can easily recognize it from the weasel. However, to most people, the superficial likenesses are more obvious than the difference. The stoat is the larger animal, its head is broader and flatter and its tail is longer and *always* has a black tip. Also the fur is thicker and less slippery looking than the weasel's. Note how the lines still follow the form.

Charcoal impressions of young stoats:
they are softer and almost fluffy compared with their parents

THE OTTER

The last member of the weasel family to claim our attention, the otter has the long sinuous body of the weasel. This is especially noticeable when it is running or diving. Note also the flat head (top, right): seen full-face it has a somewhat lugubrious expression. Below is a young dog-otter.

The otter's resemblance to its cousins can be seen again above, but the tail is long and tapering.

The head too is flatter and wider and more dog-like.

Its eyes are round and somewhat protruding.

Left: the otter in its favourite pose. Note how the lines help the form.

Note also the flatness of the head and its doglike structure and the feet, webbed with short, sharp claws.

With the otter, as with any animal, swift line drawings will be very useful. Even with these the form can be shown. The one on the left shows the undulating and curved back and that below, a certain rotundity, though neither drawing has any tone.

How form can be influenced by the direction of line.
Here rotundity and solidity were aimed at
and the sleek sinousness ignored.
All the drawings on pages 31-33 were made
with a Wolff's carbon pencil

c

Drawings made 'on the spot' and worked over later with lamp black water and a brush.
This is an excellent medium for brief sketches without surface markings and detail.

THE RABBIT

HAVING dealt with some of the less noticeable of the countryside's animals, let us take a look at the most common. One can see rabbits almost anywhere. In fact it would be a good subject to start your sketching from life. Because of its ubiquity, I was tempted to start this book with studies of the rabbit, but abandoned the idea in favour of the badger for reasons already stated.

As with other animals, try to see the major planes. The figures below show the major planes accentuated. There is quite a deep depression each side of the head between the cheek and top of the skull.

For quick sketching, line drawings are very suitable. It is possible, as I have tried to show, to suggest muscular content and solidity by pure line.

These drawings of mature rabbits were made with a soft pencil, those on the opposite page with charcoal

Charcoal is soft and easily dusted off. It is an excellent medium for a beginner who has had a little experience of pencil first. Mass effects can be achieved quickly and easily and by rubbing lightly with the finger one gets a pleasant granulated effect that suggests soft fur.

Do not overdo the line drawing : it requires some experience and for the beginner it is better to try and draw in mass. After all, line is only a convention. A mark to denote where one mass touches another. What one actually sees is not a line but one *tone* in juxtaposition with another. However, line drawings are very useful for getting down a quick vivid impression of a moving figure.

Let your line be a *moving* one, vigorous and firm. Avoid this :

39

THE HARE

A full grown hare

IT MIGHT be as well to note a few details relevant to the hare at this point. The common or brown hare is a much larger and heavier animal than the rabbit. Not only are its legs longer, but its hind-legs are very much longer than its front legs. Hence its capacity to run up hill faster than it can run down hill.

Its head is rounder, its ears longer and tipped with black and its eyes much fuller than those of the rabbit. Its eyes are set so that it can see backward better than forward. These three drawings were made in charcoal.

A leveret
about two days old

A hare startled from its form

40

THE RED SQUIRREL

IN the southern counties of Britain the red squirrel
seems to have taken the same path as the pine-martin
and pole-cat, but it can still be found in the
west and north.
In this drawing I have tried to demonstrate how your line can give solidity
and suggest the underlying structure.
And how a line can, just as easily,
give an appearance of lightness
and fineness with nothing
beyond it, as in the
bushy tail.

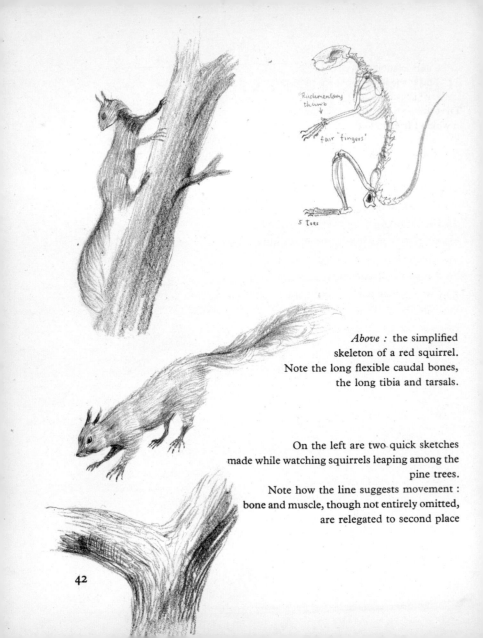

Rudimentary
thumb

four "fingers"

5 toes

Above : the simplified
skeleton of a red squirrel.
Note the long flexible caudal bones,
the long tibia and tarsals.

On the left are two quick sketches
made while watching squirrels leaping among the
pine trees.
Note how the line suggests movement :
bone and muscle, though not entirely omitted,
are relegated to second place

Two more-elaborate sketches.
The one at the lower right shows
the beast in a characteristic pose.
The other two are quick sketches again
in which I tried to find
form with as little tone as possible

This shows the general difference in shape.
The grey squirrel is leaner, more rat-like and his tail less bushy
than the red squirrel's.

Head of a grey squirrel :
note the difference in the shape of the head
and the absence of ear tufts

THE GREY SQUIRREL

FROM the farmer's point of view (and perhaps the naturalist's) the grey squirrel is a menace that should be destroyed, but it is quite an interesting animal to draw.

It has a habit of ' freezing '—stopping suddenly and staying motionless—which is extremely helpful to the artist. Young ones, too, will play and feed a few yards from an observer. The colour blends very well with that of the the tree trunks, as the small figure on the opposite page (lower left) will perhaps demonstrate. The grey squirrel frequents deciduous woods, not the pine plantations beloved of the red squirrel.

With the exception of the skeleton on page 42, all drawings of both red and grey squirrels were made with a Wolff's carbon pencil 2B.

THE FOX

THE SKELETON of a fox is very much like that of a dog. It walks on its toes and also has five toes on the forefeet and four on the hind feet, with non-retractile claws.

Its head, too, is dog-like, large and broad with a long pointed nose. It is this sharp nose together with the sudden broadening of the face and the slanting eyes that give it that essentially sly, cunning look. On the next page I have tried to sketch in those very significant lines that are essentially ' foxy '.

Foxes vary somewhat in size according to locality. Those I have seen in Cornwall and hilly country seem to be longer-legged and heavier of shoulder than elsewhere.

A pencil-and-wash sketch of a young dog-fox. Draw the animal first in pencil, showing the structure and tone, then put a wash of local colour over the top. Or you can reverse the process: put on your wash first and when it is dry do your drawing with a pencil on top.

Right : in this position notice how the body falls away, thinning at the hips. When disturbed, a fox will often trot thirty yards or so and then stop and look back over his shoulder, grinning.

Opposite page : This is a drawing in black and white Conté chalk on buff paper. This is a more messy medium than pencil and requires more care. I started with an outline, marking more strongly the build-up of the major masses, then concentrated on each mass.

46

THE WILD CAT

HERE are pencil drawings of the last of the really feral animals of Britain. The British wild cat is usually larger than our domesticated cat, has a much larger bullet-shaped head with the ears larger and set lower down and the tail is thick, ringed and always ends in a club.

The markings, too, are always of the tiger type, Sometimes the stripes are broken into dots, especially on the thighs, but the pattern is never of the blotchy sort that so many of our domestic tabbies have.

Red deer and, lower left, roe deer, in Conté on grey sugar paper.

DEER

THE DRAWINGS on page 49 were made with Conté chalks and charcoal. The red deer was drawn first in charcoal which was lightly rubbed in to give a smooth hide-like surface.

The deeper tones were put in with black Conté and white was used for the high-lights and local colour markings. This medium is useful for tone and silhouette drawings. The paper used was grey sugar-paper.

FALLOW DEER

THE DRAWINGS of fallow deer on the opposite page were all made with a carbon pencil : 1, shows the start and 2, the completed sketch. Figure 3 is really an initial sketch carried a stage further than 1. Having marked out the main structural lines and masses one can delineate the extent of local colour before completing the tone value and form.

Figure 4 is a drawing of a head of a doe, and 5 is that of a fawn. Incidentally the male of the red deer is known as a stag, the female a hind and the young a calf. The male of the fallow deer is a buck, the female a doe and the young a fawn.

1

2

4

3

5

51

Head of a viper.
The eye has a vertical pupil like a cat'

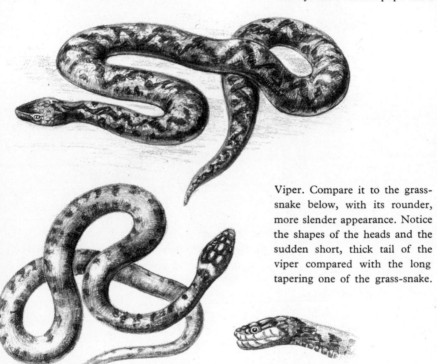

Viper. Compare it to the grass-snake below, with its rounder, more slender appearance. Notice the shapes of the heads and the sudden short, thick tail of the viper compared with the long tapering one of the grass-snake.

Head of a grass-snake. The pupil of the eye is round.

SNAKES

ON THE opposite page are drawings of the two snakes most commonly found in Britain, the viper and the grass-snake. I have not included the smooth-snake as the method of drawing it is similar and it is something of a rarity.

Previously, I postulated a cylinder as the basic form for drawing a weasel. This same concept is equally applicable to a snake, for the latter is just one long cylinder of varying diameters. Remember this and when drawing the patterning, make it conform to the contour : it will help the form.

Of course, a snake is not a true cylinder : its section would not make a circle but something like This is discernible in the drawings opposite : note how the form is retained when one coil overlaps another. By lightening the top of the uppermost coil and darkening it just before and after crossing, one gets a shallow hoop-like effect.

FROGS AND TOADS

THE DRAWINGS opposite are again in charcoal and Conté on grey paper. The method of drawing was the same : charcoal rubbed lightly in and the detail put in on top with black and white chalk. Note the difference in the skin of the toad from that of the frog.

As one can see by the sketches of their skeletons, toads and frogs are ribless animals. They have therefore, a singularly flaccid, pulpy appearance. This is even more remarkable in the toad than in the frog, for the latter has a differently shaped hip-bone. The projections from the vertebrae that form the hip, extend backwards and slightly upwards as well, above the single caudle bone that forms the tail. This accounts for that hump-backed appearance frogs possess. In the toad, however, the hip projections extend downwards and the tail protrudes slightly above them.

BATS

HERE WE have four fairly representative bats of the twelve species that breed in Britain. Below, 1, is the largest known as the noctule or great bat while 2, is the smallest and commonest, the pipistrelle. Figure 3 is the serotine, in Britain found only in Sussex and Kent : I have included it for I think it is most mouse-like of all the bats. Figures 4 and 5 are drawings of the greater horseshoe bat, so called from the leaf-like appendage upon its nose.

A bat has a furry body and wings that vary from a leathery appearance to a soft velvet. It is important to try and show the difference in texture

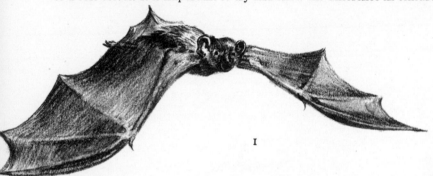

I

of wing, body and the bones of the ' hand ' by using different strokes of your pencil for each.

These were all drawn with a carbon pencil, with the exception of 5, which was lightly sketched-in with charcoal and a wash of grey over the whole drawing. When this was dry the darker portions were placed.

2

3

4

5

HEDGEHOG

HERE WE have a different type of external covering to draw. A hedgehog is roughly oval in shape covered with numerous spines or prickles of a hard horny substance. Round the flanks and on the belly and face is coarse hair.

An abrupt, heavy sort of stroke with little nuance of tone between black and white will suggest the spiny covering. Although this dense layer is not conducive to seeing or delineating the form beneath, it should be sought and can be suggested. These two drawings were made with a 2B and a 6B pencil.

59

INSECTS

All insects have a hard horny covering known as chitin and in the beetle family it is very hard and often polished. To obtain this texture with a pencil is not difficult. More pressure must be used of course and the gradation from highest light to darkest dark is abrupt.

In the great green grass-hopper, the largest of our grass-hoppers, the appearance of chitin is softened by colour and the chief problem is to distinguish between the hard body and the wings that are leathery rather than gauzy.

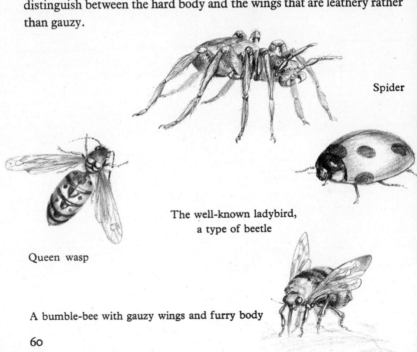

Spider

The well-known ladybird,
a type of beetle

Queen wasp

A bumble-bee with gauzy wings and furry body

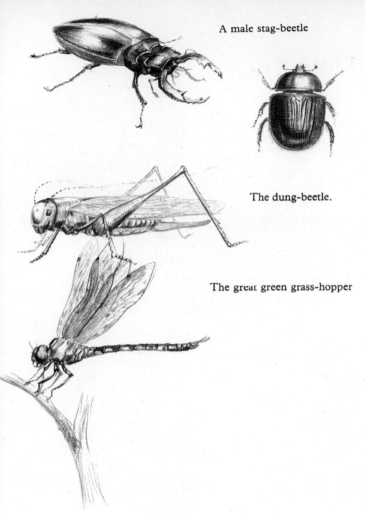

A male stag-beetle

The dung-beetle.

The great green grass-hopper

The dragon-fly.
The body is hard and brilliantly coloured and the wings gauzy.

61

CONCLUSION

I HAVE unavoidably missed out some animals, but I have made quite a comprehensive survey of the common animals of Britain. I have tried with pencil and other media to find their form and construction, to express the differences in their outer coverings : I have delineated fine and coarse hair, scales, fur and hide ; horn, skin, chitin and shell.

I have laid down no hard and fast rules. I do not think there are any. I

Watervoles, commonly and erroneously called water-rats.
They are nothing like rats in shape or habit.

Right : a common shrew

Brown rat

Dormouse

have now and then described a method of obtaining effects. It is of course, *my* method. You will probably evolve better ones.

I have, by text and example, tried to show some of the things I have learnt myself by drawing. But the symbols I have used may not be your symbols. The balance I chose between line, tone and local colour may not be your idea of what the balance should be. There is only one way to learn to draw. That is by drawing and still more drawing.

Mole : I used a 2B for the outline and shape of the head and limbs and feet. To give the impression of napless fur I used a 6B with a circular motion and then very lightly rubbed it in.

63

Lorraine

The story of
PETER
the Fisherman

by D. S. HARE

with illustrations by
ERIC WINTER

Publishers: Ladybird Books Ltd . Loughborough
© Ladybird Books Ltd (formerly Wills & Hepworth Ltd) 1970
Printed in England

PETER THE FISHERMAN

Many years ago, a man called Simon lived in a cottage by the Sea of Galilee. He was a big man, tall and strong, and a fisherman. With his brother Andrew, he sailed his fishing-boat, and the fish they caught were sold in the markets nearby.

After Simon had married, he moved to a bigger house where Andrew could stay and where his wife's mother could live as well. This was at Capernaum, a town of some size on the shore of the Sea of Galilee.

They worked with James and John, the sons of old Zebedee, and spent their days fishing, mending their nets, and keeping their boats in trim. Sometimes they fished at night.

It was a strenuous life, not one for a weakling, and dangerous too, for sudden storms would sweep down from the surrounding hills and then the sea became very rough.

4

Simon and others fishing.

0 7214 0274 7

One day a strange figure, dressed in animal skins, appeared in the district nearby. He was a prophet, and he called on the people to repent, to ask God to forgive their wrongs and to help them to turn from wicked ways. Andrew was attracted by this man's preaching, and became one of his followers.

This prophet, John, lived mainly in the desert, but preached by the River Jordan and baptised in it.

Andrew told Simon about the prophet's teaching, how John preached continually that Someone far greater than he was coming soon, God's Chosen One. Then one day John pointed out his cousin Jesus to his followers and said, "There you are; there is God's Chosen One. Follow me no more, but follow Him."

Andrew ran to tell Simon. "We have found the Messiah!" he said, and took Simon to Jesus.

John the Baptist with Andrew.

When Jesus saw Simon, He looked steadily at him and said, "So you are Simon! I am going to call you Peter, because that means 'a rock'!" Simon was puzzled, but he was at once attracted by this man who spoke with such power.

Next day Simon and Andrew went to the place of worship, the synagogue, for Jesus was preaching there. Jesus taught so well that the people were astonished. After He had preached, He healed a man sick in mind, and this amazed everyone there.

Simon invited Jesus back to his house after the service. He found that his wife's mother was very ill with a high fever. When Jesus heard this He went to see her. He took her by the hand, and at once the fever left her. She felt so much better that she got up and helped to fetch the supper for their guests.

8   *Jesus heals Simon's mother-in-law.*

That evening all the sick people of the village came to Jesus, for they had heard about Him curing a man in the synagogue. Simon watched with wonder as Jesus healed every one of the sick people.

Eventually Jesus returned to the house, tired out. He spent the night at Simon's house, but in the morning His room was empty. Simon searched everywhere and went through the town but could not find Him.

Others were now looking for this wonderful healer and teacher. Then they saw Him up on the hillside alone. They scrambled up and found Him praying.

"We have been looking for You everywhere," they said. "You must not leave us."

"I must," said Jesus. "I must go and preach the good news of the Kingdom of God in other places as well."

Then He left Capernaum.

The people find Jesus alone on a hill-top.

Simon Peter now had much to think about! This man, so calm and yet so bold, with His amazing power of healing – who was He? Was He the promised Messiah, God's Chosen One?

One day Simon was cleaning his net. He and Andrew, together with James and John, had been fishing all night long, but they had not caught a single fish.

Suddenly they saw a crowd of people heading towards the sea-shore. They were all following Jesus, but there were so many that they were not all able to hear Him. Jesus told them to sit down on the sloping bank of the sea-shore. Then He went over to Simon's boat, and climbed into the bow.

"Push out a little from the shore!" He called to Simon. So He taught the people from the boat, and they all heard Him.

12   *Jesus preaches to the crowd from the bow of Simon's boat.*

"Thank you, Simon Peter," said Jesus as He climbed out of the boat. "Now go out and catch some fish!"

Simon sighed. "Master," he replied, "we have been fishing all night and we have caught nothing." Jesus smiled at him. "Go and try now," He said, and Simon did as Jesus told him.

Andrew and Simon pushed off into deep water and, expecting nothing, let down their nets. Soon these were sagging, for they had made a huge catch. They started to haul in the nets, but there were so many fish that the nets began to break. They called to James and John to come and help them, for the catch was so heavy.

Simon was amazed and a little frightened. When they reached the shore, Simon ran and knelt before Jesus saying, "Leave me, Lord, I am only a sinful man."

Jesus replied, "Do not be afraid, Simon. From now on you will go fishing for men who will follow Me."

Andrew and Simon make a huge catch.

So Peter, as we must now call him, left his fishing and became a full-time disciple. He followed Jesus on His preaching tours around Galilee. Soon, about seventy people were with Jesus, for in every town more followers joined them.

One day on a mountain side, Jesus called twelve of his followers to Him. He told them they were to be His chosen disciples. Peter was among them. He listened attentively as Jesus taught them about His Kingdom of Love, where people would respect others as much as themselves and seek God's way and God's will rather than their own.

This inspiring message was eagerly accepted by the Jewish country people. They had a hard life because they were ruled by a bad king, Herod, and also by the Romans, who had conquered Palestine and demanded extra taxes.

16   *Jesus calls twelve apostles.*

Once an important synagogue ruler, named Jairus, came running to Jesus. "Come quickly, please," he said, "my little daughter is dying. Come and heal her." Jesus praised the man's faith and, followed by a large crowd, went with him.

On the way, a servant came and said to Jairus, "Your daughter has died. Do not trouble the Master any more." Jesus heard the message. "Do not be afraid," He said, "just have faith."

At Jairus' house, Jesus called Peter, James and John into the room with the girl's parents. Peter wondered what Jesus could do, for she lay dead in her bed.

Peter watched Jesus take her hand and gently say, "Get up, my child." The girl stirred, got up and walked about. They were all amazed. Peter could hardly realise that Jesus had actually given new life to the girl.

"Now," Jesus reminded them, "she will need something to eat."

18   *Jesus brings Jairus' daughter back to life.*

One afternoon, a huge crowd of about five thousand people was listening to Jesus at a quiet place on the shore. When evening came, Peter wanted Jesus to send them away to buy their food. Jesus replied, "They need not go away; you give them something to eat." Peter thought He must be joking. "We have only five rolls and a couple of fish," he replied. "How can we feed these thousands?"

Then Jesus told him to make the people sit in groups. He prayed over the few rolls and the fish, and told the disciples to give them out. To their astonishment, the supply never ran short; they were able to feed everyone. In fact, there were enough pieces left over to fill a dozen baskets.

The people, filled and satisfied now, went home. And Jesus went off to the hills alone, to pray.

Jesus feeds the multitude.

Jesus had told the disciples to sail across the Sea of Galilee in their boat. So they climbed in and set sail across the water. They did not question Jesus, they just obeyed.

Night came, and the wind began to increase. The sea became rough and rowing was hard, for the wind was against them. By this time they were far from the shore, struggling in the dark against the sea and the wind.

Suddenly they saw the figure of a man near them on the water. "It is a ghost!" cried one, terrified.

"Do not be afraid," called Jesus. "It is I. Have courage!" Then they recognised Him. It really was Jesus, walking towards them on the water.

"Lord," said Peter, "can I come to You on the water?"

"Come along!" said Jesus. So Peter, looking straight at Jesus, began to walk across the water towards Him.

The disciples see Jesus walking on the water.

Suddenly Peter felt frightened. He took his eyes off Jesus, looked down at the waves and began to sink.

"Lord, save me!" he cried out. Jesus reached out His hand and caught him.

"You must not doubt, but have faith," He said. Jesus and Peter joined the others in the boat and soon they were at the shore. "Truly, You are the Son of God," they all said.

Peter was learning a great many things by being with Jesus, but the most important was to trust the Lord completely. Jesus had not only taught His disciples about the Kingdom of God, but had also shown that God cares for each and every one of His children.

By giving life to a dead girl, feeding hungry thousands, and now walking over the water, He had shown both the power and the love of God.

Peter walks to Jesus on the water.

Peter was regarded by the other disciples as their leader. He found himself keeping in order the crowds who flocked to hear Jesus and to be healed by Him.

One day a crowd of children clustered around Jesus. "Get back, you youngsters," ordered Peter. "Can't you see the Master's tired out, and doesn't want you clamouring around Him?" And he began to turn them away.

But Jesus restrained him, saying, "Let the children all come to Me; don't stop them." So they came around Him, held His hand, and sat on His lap.

"Children," He said to His disciples, "are so trusting. And I say to you that unless you receive the Kingdom of God with child-like trust, you shall never enter it."

Peter felt ashamed, and wished that he hadn't been so quick to speak; but he had learnt another lesson from the Master.

Jesus calls children to Him.

By this time Peter had been with Jesus for nearly three years, travelling all over northern Palestine, teaching, preaching and healing. Now Jesus set out for Jerusalem.

One evening He talked to His disciples about going away from them, and yet not entirely leaving them. Then He took a towel and a basin, and solemnly went around to each man and washed his feet. Peter was horrified – this was a slave's work, not for his Master to do. He did not want Jesus to wash his feet.

"Not me, Lord!" he cried.

But Jesus answered, "If I do not wash you, Peter, you cannot be one of Mine."

"Then wash me all over, Lord," said Peter hastily. But Jesus just washed his feet. He said He had given them all an example.

"It is no good talking about loving other people," He explained, "without showing it in loving service to others."

28   *Jesus washes Peter's feet.*

Jesus told His disciples that He would be betrayed, and then He would go to a place where they could not follow. Peter was indignant.

"Why cannot I follow you, Lord?" he said. "I would die for You!"

"Would you?" said Jesus. "I tell you that this night, before the cock crows twice for the dawn, you will disown Me three times."

As they talked and prayed in the Garden that dark evening, a group of men approached. Their leader was Judas, a disciple. He greeted Jesus with a kiss, and then the soldiers with him seized Jesus.

Peter immediately grabbed a sword, struck out at a man and cut off his ear, but Jesus gently rebuked him.

"Put away your sword, Peter," He said. "It is not needed." He healed the man's ear, then was led away.

Peter followed at a distance, until Jesus was taken inside.

The arrest of Jesus.

Peter felt cold, so he went over to the open fire in the courtyard to warm himself. A servant girl looked closely at him and said, "Were you not with the man from Galilee – with Jesus?"

"No," replied Peter, "I do not know Him." As he walked away, a cock crowed.

The maid-servant told the others, "I am sure he is one of them." "No! I am not!" shouted Peter.

The others said, "You must be; you are from Galilee, too!"

Peter replied angrily, "I tell you, I do not know this man!" Then a cock crowed a second time, reminding Peter of Jesus' words. He went away and wept bitterly.

As daylight came, there was urgent activity everywhere. Peter was told that three criminals were to be crucified – nailed alive to a large cross of wood. Then he learned with horror that one of the three was to be his own Lord and Master – Jesus.

Peter's denial.

Peter watched the Roman soldiers assemble and march off with the prisoners, each prisoner carrying his own cross. What a terrible end, he thought, for his loving, kind Master – to die like a criminal.

On a hill outside the city wall, first the two criminals, then Jesus between them, were nailed to the huge crosses. Peter watched with a heavy heart for as long as he could, and then went back to the other disciples.

He found them all afraid, downcast, upset. Soon the women came back, together with John. They had been comforting Mary, Jesus' mother. They told Peter that Jesus was dead, and that although it was only mid-afternoon, it was as dark as night outside.

That evening the women took precious ointments to wash the body of Jesus. It had been taken down from the cross and placed in a special tomb in the hillside by a man called Joseph. Then the entrance was sealed with a huge rock. As the next day was the Sabbath, or Day of Rest, they remained indoors.

The Crucifixion.

At dawn on the day after the Sabbath, Peter was praying. Suddenly Mary Magdalene rushed in, very upset. "I have just been to the tomb," she said breathlessly. "The stone has been rolled away, and the body is not there!"

Peter immediately ran to the tomb. Inside, he saw only the linen cloth that had been wrapped around the body. He walked back puzzled, deep in thought, leaving Mary weeping at the tomb.

Soon after, Mary Magdalene hurried in. "I have seen the Lord!" she exclaimed to their startled ears. "He is alive – and I have talked with Him!" But they did not believe her.

That evening, the disciples met behind locked doors. Suddenly they realised that Jesus was with them; He was there, talking to them, explaining that He had overcome death, encouraging them to believe and trust in Him.

Peter grasped the feet and hands of Jesus. "It really is You, Lord!" he exclaimed.

The empty tomb.

Jesus told Peter to return to Galilee and wait for Him there.

One evening, by the lakeside, Peter suddenly announced: "I am going fishing." "We will join you," said the others. So they went out and fished all night, but caught nothing.

As dawn broke, a man on the shore called to them, "Have you caught anything?" When they said they had not, he replied, "Throw out your net on the other side!" They did so – and caught so many fish that they were unable to pull in the net. John said to Peter, "Surely it is the Lord!"

Peter jumped into the water and hurried to the shore. Jesus had a fire ready for cooking their breakfast. They were amazed and said little. Then Jesus turned to Peter.

"Do you really love me, Simon Peter?" He asked.

"Yes, Lord," replied Peter.

"Then," said Jesus, "feed My flock."

Peter's miraculous catch.

Jesus had meant that Peter was to look after the believers, the first Christians, and to give up his fishing. So they returned to Jerusalem, and a little while later they all met on a hill called the Mount of Olives, outside the city. There it was that Jesus came to them for the last time.

"Now I must return to My Father," He said, "but you will receive a Power within you, the Spirit of God, which My Father will send you. Then you must spread My teaching, not only here in Jerusalem, not only in Palestine, but throughout the whole world."

When He had said this He seemed to be taken up in front of their eyes until a cloud hid Him from their sight. Then two angels stood by them and assured them that although they would not see Jesus again, He would always be with them.

Full of hope and new courage, the disciples went back to the city, aware that they would no longer see Jesus in person, but eagerly awaiting God's gift of the Holy Spirit.

The Ascension.

On the next festival day, Peter was praying with the disciples when suddenly the whole room was full of a rushing, mighty wind, and it seemed as if flames of fire were present upon every person. But each one knew that God was with him – and each was filled with God's Spirit.

Peter led the disciples outside, and they began to speak to the crowds. The people were amazed. "We all come from many different lands," they said, "but we can each hear in our own language."

Then Peter told them that God had sent His Holy Spirit to dwell within them, as He had promised, and this could happen now because Jesus, whom they had crucified, had been raised up by God to be their Lord.

Some Jews did not understand this, but three thousand asked to be baptised, showing that they were true believers in Jesus.

42   *Pentecost – preaching to the crowds.*

One afternoon Peter and John went to the Temple to pray. There was a beggar sitting at the gate who had been lame all his life. He asked Peter and John to give him something.

"I have no money," said Peter, "but what I have I will give you. In the name of Jesus Christ – walk!"

He helped the beggar to stand up. The man felt strength in his ankles and began to walk. He went into the Temple to give thanks to God. Afterwards he began to leap about, so excited was he at the thrill of walking. The people came running to see, for they recognised the man, now jumping for joy, as the crippled beggar.

Peter spoke to the crowd. "It is faith in Jesus which has cured this man," he said.

Many became believers; but Peter and John were arrested by the Temple guards.

The lame beggar is healed.

Peter and John were brought before the Council of the High Priest. They were forbidden to teach another word about Jesus.

But Peter replied, "Is it right for us to listen to what you say, rather than what God says? For we cannot help telling others what we have seen with our own eyes." After a warning, they were released.

Still they continued to preach, for they knew that God wanted them to proclaim His message despite opposition. And opposition there was. On a number of occasions they were arrested, imprisoned and beaten.

Some time later King Herod ordered that James, brother of John, should be put to death. When he saw that this pleased the Jews, he imprisoned Peter. But the believers prayed earnestly to God to save Peter. One night while Peter was asleep with soldiers on guard at the door, an angel appeared in the cell.

Peter in prison.

"Get up quickly," the angel said to Peter.

Peter's chains fell off, and when the angel told him to put on his sandals and cloak, he did so automatically, as if in a dream.

"Follow me," said the angel, and led Peter right past the guards and out of prison. Then they reached the big iron gate leading out to the city. It opened for them and the angel vanished. Peter was free! He realised then that God had sent the angel to rescue him.

He went to the house where the Christians met, and knocked on the door.

"Who is there?" called the girl who came to answer.

"It is Peter," he replied. She was so surprised that she ran in to the others without opening the door, saying Peter was there. "You are crazy!" they said.

But soon they realised that she was right. They welcomed Peter with great joy.

Peter's miraculous release from prison.

Gradually the group of believers in Jerusalem grew in number. The confident faith and assurance of the disciples helped others to believe that Jesus really was the Son of God, and that trusting Him gave them a new and better kind of life. Peter was one of the leaders of these believers, the founders of our Christian faith.

But Peter felt that he must take the Gospel message to other lands, too. He travelled more, preaching to the Jews wherever he found them.

Eventually he went to Rome, and there he suffered persecution and death, as his Master had done. On the orders of the Emperor Nero, very many Christians were put to death in Rome, and Peter was amongst them.

Some writers say that Peter asked to be crucified head down, as he was not worthy to die in the same way as his Master. Peter had been Jesus' faithful friend and disciple, a steadfast, rocklike apostle to his life's end.

Peter before Nero in Rome.

Series 522